Moving

Karen Bryant-Mole

Heinemann Library
Chicago, Illinois

First published by Heinemann Interactive Library,
an imprint of Reed Educational & Professional Publishing,
Chicago, Illinois

Customer Service 888-454-2279

Visit our website at www.heinemannlibrary.com

Printed and bound in Hong Kong
Designed by Jean Wheeler
Commissioned photography by Zul Mukhida
Consultant—Hazel Grice

© BryantMole Books 1998

06 05 04 03 02
10 9 8 7 6 5 4 3 2 1

Library of Congress Cataloging-in-Publication Data
Bryant-Mole, Karen.
    Moving / by Karen Bryant-Mole.
        p.   cm. -- (Science all around me)
    Includes bibliographical references and index.
    Summary: Briefly explains the scientific principles of animal
movement.
    ISBN 1-57572-630-0 (lib. bdg.)   ISBN 1-4034-0054-7 (pbk. bdg.)
    1. Animal locomotion--Juvenile literature. 2. Plants-
-Irritability and movements--Juvenile literature.   [1. Animal
locomotion.]   I. Title. II. Series.
QP301.B894   1998
573.7'9--dc21   97-41944
                                                               CIP
                                                                AC

A number of questions are posed in this book. They are designed to consolidate children's understanding by encouraging further exploration of the science in their everyday lives.

Acknowledgments
The Publishers would like to thank the following for permission to reproduce photographs: Bruce Coleman p. 8 (Gunther Ziesler), p. 18 (J. Brackenbury), p. 20 (Jane Burton); Eye Ubiquitous p. 14 (Steve Lindridge); Positive Images pp. 12, 22; Tony Stone Images p. 4 (Daryl Balfour), p. 10 (James Balog); Zefa pp. 6, 16.

Every effort has been made to contact copyright holders of any material reproduced in this book. Any omissions will be rectified in subsequent printings if notice is given to the Publisher.

Words that appear in the text in **bold** can be found in the glossary.

Contents

Animals   4

Skeleton   6

Joints   8

Muscles   10

Air, Land, and Water   12

Flying   14

Swimming   16

Legs   18

Moving without Legs   20

Plants   22

More Books to Read   24

Glossary   24

Index   24

Animals

All animals can move. They need to move to find food to eat and somewhere safe to rest.

They may need to **escape** from other animals. This elephant had to move to find the water it is drinking.

(i) *Human beings are animals, too.*

See for yourself...

People and other animals can move parts of their bodies while staying in one place.

Adam moved his arm and hand to pick up this apple.

He will move his lips, teeth, and tongue while he eats it.

Skeleton

Many animals have a skeleton. A skeleton is inside the body. It is made up of bones.

A skeleton gives the body its shape and allows it to move.

? *Can you see some of the mother antelope's bones through her skin?*

See for yourself...

Carl is trying to feel his skeleton. His hands are on his ribs.

He has long bones in his arms and legs and lots of little bones in his hands and feet.

His **spine** is made up of small bones that allow his back to bend.

Joints

Animals' bones are linked together at places called joints.

Joints in this ape's arms and legs allow them to bend so the ape can climb up the tree.

(i) *Some joints let the bones move backwards and forwards. Other joints let the bones twist and turn.*

See for yourself...

Our joints let us bend and twist our bodies. Jessica is trying to bend in as many places as she can!

She is using joints in her ankles, toes, knees, and hips.

She is also using joints in her fingers, wrists, elbows, shoulders, and neck.

Muscles

Bones do not move by themselves. They are pulled into different positions by **muscles**. The more a muscle is used, the stronger it becomes.

This tiger does a lot of running and jumping. It has large, strong leg muscles.

 Muscles can only pull. They cannot push.

See for yourself...

Some of our muscles are large and some are very small.

Melissa can feel the large muscles in her arm pulling as she lifts up this heavy bag.

Lots of tiny muscles in her face are making a big smile!

Air, Land, and Water

The type of body an animal has depends on how and where it moves.

These ducks use their legs and feet to walk on land and swim through water. They use their wings to fly through the air.

(i) *Ducks have special feet called webbed feet. These help them to swim.*

See for yourself...

Brian is putting some model animals into groups.

One group of animals moves on land. One group can fly through the air. The other group can swim through water.

Flying

Almost all birds can fly. They fly by flapping their wings or by gliding.

Flapping helps to push the bird through the air.

Gliding is like floating on the air. Instead of flapping its wings, the bird keeps them stretched out.

? *Can you think of any birds that can't fly?*

See for yourself...

Birds' wings are a special shape.

They make the air move more quickly over the top of the wings than underneath. This helps lift the bird into the air.

Kate is testing this by blowing along the top of a strip of paper. As she blows, the paper lifts up.

Swimming

Fish swim by moving their tails from side to side. This pushes the fish through the water.

Many fish have **fins** on their bodies. These fins allow the fish to **steer** in the direction it wants to go.

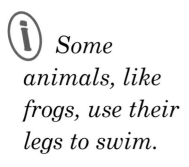 *Some animals, like frogs, use their legs to swim.*

See for yourself...

Jonathan is using a wind-up bath toy to see how a flapping tail can push a fish through water.

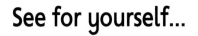

He has wound up the bath toy and put it in the water. As the tail flaps from side to side, the bath toy moves forwards.

Legs

This young **locust** uses its legs to jump from place to place. Kangaroos and frogs also move by jumping.

Other animals use their legs to run or walk.

Some, like tortoises, move slowly. Others, like cheetahs, can move very quickly.

? *What other animals move quickly?*

Kate is counting all the ways she can use her legs to move from one place to another.

She has hopped, run, walked, jumped, and skipped.

Now she is crawling.

19

Moving without Legs

This earthworm moves by squishing up and stretching out different **sections** of its body.

Many snakes wriggle along the ground by bending to one side and then the other.

(i) *Earthworms have lots of tiny bristles under their bodies, which help them to grip the earth.*

See for yourself...

Snails slide along on a strong muscle.

Melissa has put a snail into a small plastic tank. She is watching the snail as it moves up the side.

If you try this, remember to put the snail back where you found it.

Plants

Plants can move parts of themselves, too.

Some plants close up their petals at night.
This photograph was taken in the evening.
The plants are just starting to close up their petals.

Some plants also close up their petals when it is cold or wet.

See for yourself...

Green plants need sunlight to make food for themselves.

Adam put this plant on a windowsill for a few days. Now all the leaves are facing in the same direction.

They moved themselves into this position so they could catch as much sunlight as possible.

Glossary

bristles   short hairs

escape   get away from something

fins   flaps that stick out

locust   a type of insect

muscles   bundles of thin bands that move parts of the body

sections   parts of something

spine   backbone

steer   go in a chosen direction

More Books to Read

Ganeri, Anita. *Moving.* Chatham, NJ: Raintree Steck-Vaughn. 1994.

Lantier-Sampon, Patricia. *Wings.* Milwaukee: Gareth Stevens. 1994.

Rauzon, Mark J. *Feet, Flippers, Hooves, & Hands.* New York: Lothrop, Lee & Shepard Books. 1994.

Index

animals 4–6, 8, 12–14, 16,18, 20–21

bending 8–9

birds 14–15

bones 6–8, 10

climbing 8

crawling 19

fins 16

fish 16–17

flying 12–15

joints 8–9

jumping 10, 18, 19

legs 18–19

movement in,

air 12–15

land 12–13

water 4, 12–13, 16-17

muscles 10–11, 21

plants 22–23

running 10, 18, 19

skeletons 6–7

swimming 12, 13, 16–17

walking 12, 18, 19